New Zealand Journey

A
Travel Colouring
Book
for Adults

Created by Susan Dathweston

Published by Kotare Publishing in 2015
First Edition; First Printing

Illustrations and design Kotare

Http://kotarepublishing

ISBN 978-0-9967716-0-3

A NEW ZEALAND JOURNEY

Explore thisbeautiful country

RELAXATION COLOURING
for
BEGINNER to ADVANCED
COLOURISTS

This book is dedicated to the amazing people around the world who stand up to protect and care for animals.

A big thank you to *Ricky Gervais* whose dedication to raging against animal abuse has made, and continues to make, such a difference in the world!

Welcome to a colouring journey around Aotearoa, New Zealand

Colour your way around the "Land of the Long White Cloud".
Scan the QR codes for more information, social media pages
and prizes

Colour Relaxation

Colouring has been proven to be an effective way of relaxing body and mind. By relieving stress in the body you can also set up the optimal conditions for weight loss, anxiety relief and sound sleep.

Besides that ... it's just plain fun!

Join us on an exploration of beautiful New Zealand and let the rhythm of colouring help you to a happier more relaxed state.

All designs are purposely blank on the reverse to avoid colour bleed through.

When you're not colouring, keep an eye on our Facebook and webpages too! You'll find the latest tips from expert colourists, product recommendations and discounts and you can even win a prize by uploading a picture of your latest and best colouring creation!

Follow us on Facebook at Colour-me-Happy
www.kotarepublishing.com

WELCOME TO ...

NEW ZEALAND

Nature crafted New Zealand with the surreal beauty of a movie set. Few destinations boast so many staggering natural wonders packed into such a small area. Snow-capped peaks, sparkling coves, coastal glaciers, rainforests, fjords and fish-filled rivers are some of the treasures travelers can explore. In Rotorua, oneof the world's largest geothermal areas, visitors can witness the powerful forces that birthed these landscapes in the bubbling mud ponds and hissing springs.

Thanks to its dramatic topography, New Zealand is known for adrenaline-fueled sports. White water rafting, luging, jet boating, heli-skiing, skydiving, and mountain biking round out the list of outdoor adventures and the country is home to one of the highest bungee jumps in the world. Strategically, New Zealand is a breeze to travel around. Self-drive vacations are popular and the country's diverse accomodations range from quaint bed and breakfast inns and eco-lodges to some of the world's most luxurious hotels.

Scan the QR code for beautiful photos of the destinations featured in the welcome guides.

There is an ancient wonder-tale about a huge predatory bird called the Pouakai, which the Maori said inhabited the mountains and was large enough to carry human beings off to its nest or den. The legend was probably based around the now extinct Haast's Eagle that once lived in the South Island and was the largest eagle know to have existed.

WAIHEKE ISLAND

Vineyards & Olive Groves

Waiheke Island is in the Hauraki Gulf, a half hour ferry ride from New Zealand's largest city, Auckland. Home of vineyards and olive groves, Waiheke was voted the 5th best destination in the world by Lonely Planet and the 4th best island in the world by Conde Nast.

WELCOME TO ...
COROMANDEL

Just across the Hauraki Gulf from Auckland, the rugged Coromandel Peninsula seems a world away from the city's hustle and bustle. Craggy mountains cloaked in native forest form a spine along the peninsula offering excellent opportunities for hiking and birding. Visitors can also relax on the golden beaches, sea kayak around the offshore islands, sky dive, and visit the many galleries and art studios. At Hot Water Beach a dip in the the bubbling hot pools is a great way to end a busy day of sightseeing.

Hei-tiki is an ornamental pendant of the Maori, usually made of greenstone and considered a treasure. Maori are the indigenous people of Aotearoa New Zealand and are proud of their rich cultural heritage.

A World Heritage Site, Fiordland National Park protects some of the most spectacular scenery in the country. Glaciers sculpted this dramatic landscape carving the famous fjiords of Milford, Dusky and Doubtful Sounds. Visitors here can explore gushing cascades, offshore islands, virgin rainforests, vast lakes and craggy mountain peaks. Unsurprisingly the park is a haven for hikers with some of the country's best walks including the famous Milford Track. Sea kayaking is a popular way to explore the fjiords and visitors can also enjoy a scenic flight over the park for a bird's eye view of its staggering beauty.

Orca or Killer Whales are actually the largest member of the dolphin family and are found throughout New Zealand waters. Pods of Orca are know to venture into Wellington Harbour looking for their favourite food ... stingrays! Orca can also be seen in the Gulf around such places as Waiheke Island and Half Moon Bay in Auckland.

Whales are the world's largest mammals and almost half the world's whale and dolphin species are found in New Zealand. Blue, Humpback, Southern Right and Sperm Whales are all found in our coastal waters and visitors can jump on carefully controlled whale watching boats that allow wonderful viewing while still keeping the whales safe and undisturbed.

WELCOME TO ...
BAY of ISLANDS

A three-hour drive north of Auckland, the beautiful Bay of Islands is one of the most popular vacation destinations in the country. More than 144 islands dot the glittering bay making it a haven for sailing and cruising. Penguins, dolphins, whales and marine life thrive in these fertile waters and visitors can sea kayak along the coast or hike the many island trails. Don't miss touring Cape Brett and the famous rock formation called Hole in the Rock or exploring the sub-tropical forests where Kauri trees grow. The quaint towns in the area such as Russell, Opua, Pahia and Kerikeri are great bases for exploring this scenic bay.

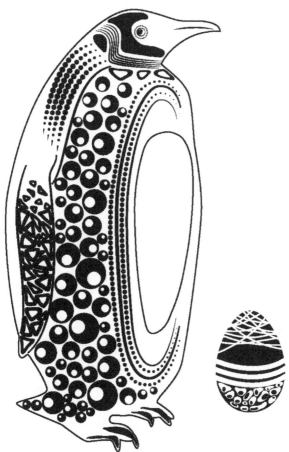

New Zealand waters are a diving paradise with accessible coastlines, marine reserves and hundreds of offshore islands creating an underwater world that is vast and diverse. The late Jacques Cousteau dived New Zealand waters often and thought that the Poor Knights Islands Marine Reserve was one of the world's top five diving locations.

New Zealand is home to 5 species of turtles. Leather back turtles have been found as far south as Fiordland and even seen in the Arctic. Green Turtles however prefer to bask in the warmer waters of the North Island and can be regularly seen at Poor Knights Island, a renowned world class dive site.

WELCOME TO ...
QUEENSTOWN

Snuggled between the shores of shimmering Lake Wakatipu and the snowy peaks of the Remarkables, Queenstown is New Zealand's adventure capital and one of the country's top destinations for international visitors. Bungee jumping, jet boating, white-water rafting, paragliding, rock climbing, mountain biking and downhill skiing are just some of the adrenaline-fueled sports on offer. Explore the stunning alpine scenery on the excellent network of hiking trails. In addition to the adventure sports, Queenstown offers all the creature comforts with first-class hotels, spas, restaurants, galleries and shops. Its also a great base for trips to the central Otago region where visitors can see gold mining towns and the Middle Earth Scenery from the popular "Lord of the Rings" movies.

A well kept secret in Taupo is the impressive set of Maori Rock Carvings at Mine Bay. They are over 10 meters (33 feet) high and only accessible by water. While they may look ancient they were actually created in the late 70's by master carver Matahi Whakataka-Brightwell as a gift to Taupo.

In the center of the North Island, a few kilometers from glittering Lake Taupo, New Zealand's largest lake, Tongariro National Park is a dual World Heritage Site due to its spectacular volcanic features and its importance to the Maori culture. In 1887, Maori chief Te Heuheu Tukino IV gifted the volcanic peaks of Tongariro, Ngauruhoe and part of Ruapehu to the people of New Zealand in order to preserve this sacred land. One of the oldest national parks in the world. Tongariro is a land of dramatic beauty with towering volcanoes, turquoise lakes, arid plateaus, alpine meadows and hot springs. A highlight of the park is the Tongariro Alpine Crossing which is one of the most popular day walks in the country.

Monarch butterflies are New Zealand's largest butterfly and have been here since the late 1800's. The Maori name for the Monarch is Kakahu and it is often seen as a spirit animal that symbolises personal transformation. How many butterflies can you find? Post to our Facebook page for a chance to win a prize.

WELCOME TO ...
ROTORUA

On the tumultuous Pacific Ring of Fire, Rotorua is one of the most active geothermal regions in the world. This is a land where the earth speaks. Boiling mud pools, hissing geysers, volcanic craters and steaming thermal springs betray the forces that birthed much of New Zealand's dramatic topography. Visitors can take a walking tour of these geothermal wonders, soak in steaming mineral springs and learn about the region's rich Maori history and culture. Adventure seekers will also find plenty of things to do. Sky-diving, luging and mountain biking are some of the activities on offer. Trout fishing is also popular and Rotorua is also the gateway to the ski fields of Mount Ruapehu. Nearby Wai-O-Tapu is also a popular tourist attraction with colourful hot springs and the famour Champagne Pool and Lady Know Geyser.

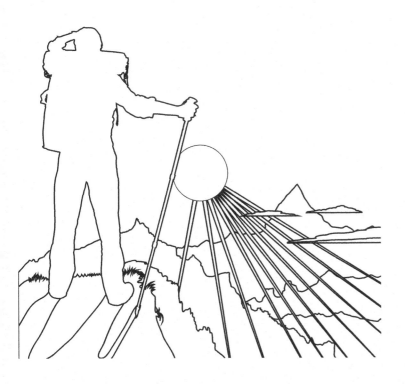

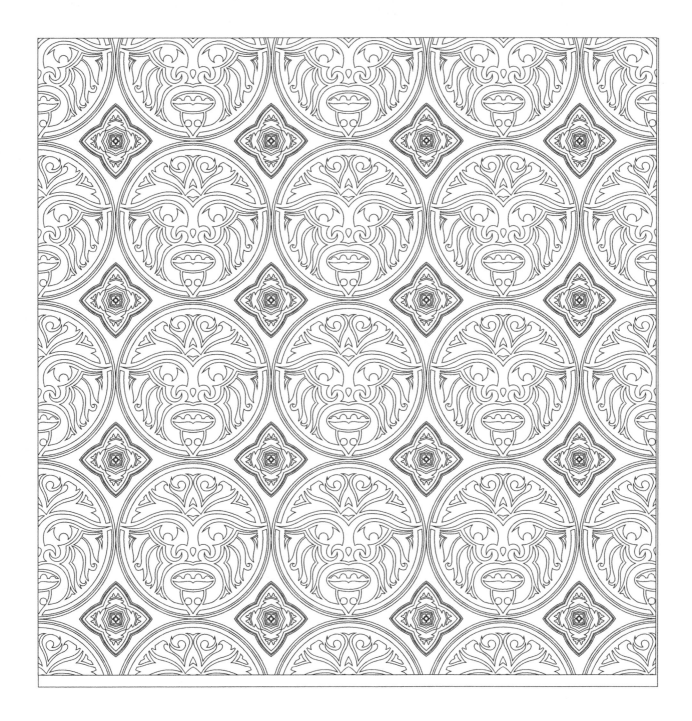

Here is a lovely design based on a stylised totem face. Most Maori carvings are not religious but usually represent the ancestors of the tribe rather than idols. If you have the chance to visit a large carved meeting house (whare runanga) you will see the most beautiful and intricate carvings.

Among the most accessible glaciers in the world, Franz Josef and Fox Glaciers are the main tourist atractions in spectacular Westland Tai Poutini National Park. Both of these rivers of ice flow from some of the highest peaks in the Southern Alps to near sea level where the gentle coastal climate makes it easy for visitors to explore them on foot. Guided hikes lead to the contorted frozen landscape of ice caves and pinnacles at the foot of the glaciers. For an aerial view, seaplanes and helicopters fly visitors to the top of these vast tongues of ice.

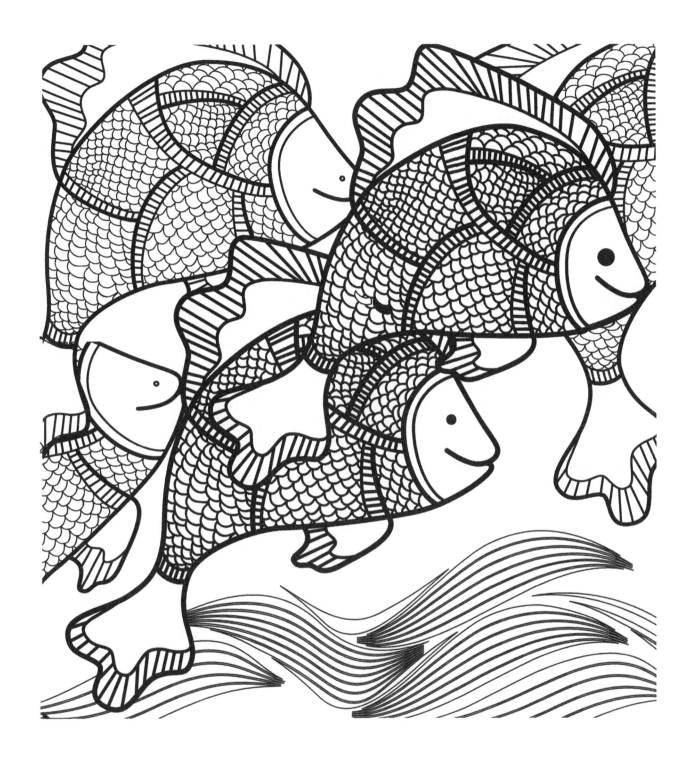

Legend has it that the country of New Zealand was fished from the sea by the daring demigod Maui. He made a magic fishhook and threw it over the side of his canoe where he hooked a huge fish. His brothers carved out pieces of fish for themselves and these are now the many valleys, mountains and rocky coastlines of the North Island.

WELCOME TO ...
ABEL TASMAN
NATIONAL PARK

The Abel Tasman Coast Track in Abel Tasman National Park is one of New Zealand's Great Walks. Winding along sparkling Tasman Bay, from Marahau to Separation Point, this scenic 51 kilometer hike lies in one of the sunniest regions of the South Island. Along the way hikers can snorkel in secluded coves, spot fur seals, dolphins, penguins and a diverse range of birds, hike through cool forests and enjoy panoramic views from the rugged coastal cliffs. Photographers will also enjoy the many weathered rock formations especially Split Apple Rock, a giant bounder sliced in two. The hike takes around three days and accommodation ranges from campgrounds and rustic huts to plush private lodges. Sea Kayaks are also a popular way to explore this beautiful coast

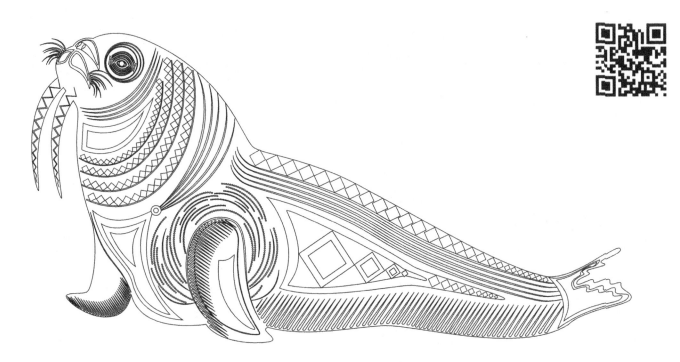

Central Otago in the South Island is renowned for its stunning displays of wild flowers which flourish along roadsides, river edges, and in valleys, hills and mountains. Countless varieties adorn landscapes in spring, summer and autumn - many of them rare and some endemic to their location.

WELCOME TO ...
AORAKI/ MT. COOK
NATIONAL PARK

In the heart of the Southern Alps, New Zealand's highest peaks rise above the alpine landscapes of Aoraki National Park, also called Mount Cook National Park. More than 40 percent of the park is covered in glaciers and the country's tallest mountain Aoraki/ Mount Cook and the longest glacier, the Tasman Glacier, lie within its borders. This a top destination for mountaineering. In fact Sir Edmund Hillary trained here for his legendary Mount Everest ascent. Nature lovers will appreciate the diversity of flora and fauna with more than 300 species of alpine plants and 40 species of birds. Mount Cook Village is a great base for exploring the park and enjoying scenic flights, ski touring, heli-skiing, hunting, hiking and stargazing trips.

New Zealand is known for its sheep farming but if you're not from NZ, you may not have heard of the cartoon strip "Footrot Flats". Scan the QR code to discover the adventures of the iconic "Dog" and his owner "Wal".

WELCOME TO ...

AUCKLAND

Blessed with two sparkling harbours, Auckland, the "City of Sails", is New Zealand's largest city and the most populous Polynesian city in the world. Blonde and black sand beaches, rainforest hiking trails, picturesque coves, islands and volcanoes surround the city making it a perfect base for day trips and wilderness adventures. To really appreciate Auckland's stunning location visitors can zoom up the 328 meter Sky Tower for spectacular views across the city and hinterland. Auckland is also home to top-notch dining, a vibrant arts scene and a revamped waterfront district packed with boutiques and restaurants.

The Silvereye, also known as the Waxeye, is a tiny bird found throughout the country. Its Maori name, tauhou, means stranger or more literally 'new arrival'. Highly entertaining, it sometimes hovers like a humming bird. They can be enticed into gardens by various treats and love to hang upside down on a ball of lard or dripping!

WELCOME TO ...
KAIKOURA

Birders, wildlife enthusiasts and seafood afficionados will love the charming coastal village of Kaikoura. Tucked between the Seaward Kaikoura Range and the Pacific Ocean, Kaikoura offers excellent coastal hikes and popular whale watching tours. In addition to Sperm whales and Humpbacks, passengers may also see fur seals, dolphins and a wide variety of birds including the graceful albatross. Kaikoura is also renowned for its fresh caught crayfish, mussels and other seafood delights.

This is a great mandala for the advanced colourist. The design celebrates the Kiwi love of the ocean. Whether it be swimming, rowing or sailing, New Zealanders have been world leaders in the nautical field but champion or not, all Kiwi's love being on, in or under the ocean.

New Zealand boasts an amazing and diverse number of bird species, several of which are only found here. They include the Kiwi, the Tui, the Blue Duck, the Kaka and the Kakapo. The Kakapo (night parrot) is one of our unique treasures with less than 130 surviving birds, however an extensive breed and release programme is in place in an effort to boost the population.

We hope you enjoyed our colouring tour of
New Zealand and that perhaps you may even
be inspired to visit this beautiful country.

For Chevvy ...
our old and loving hound